Adventures in Seeking Knowledge

Adventures in Seeking Knowledge

Rose Hale

Copyright © 2019, Rose Hale

All rights reserved. Printed in the U.S.A.

No part of this publication may be reproduced or transmitted in any form or by any means, electronic or mechanical, including photocopy, recording or any information storage and retrieval system now known or to be invented, without permission in writing from the publisher, except by a reviewer who wishes to quote brief passages in connection with a review written for inclusion in a magazine, newspaper or broadcast.

Published in the United States
by eBooks2go, Inc.
1827 Walden Office Square, Suite 260, Schaumburg, IL 60173

ISBN-10: 1-5457-4808-X
ISBN-13: 978-1-5457-4808-4

Library of Congress Cataloging in Publication

Adventures in Seeking Knowledge

is dedicated to those who have taught me to love God's words and to all who have encouraged me in my writing journey. I'm forever grateful for all of you.

My life verse is Luke 1:49 "For the Mighty One has done great things for me; and holy is His name." My prayer is that you see that verse reflected in these pages.

Contents

Introduction
1. Anger: Proverbs 17:27
2. Ask: Proverbs 2:6
3. Bible: 2 Timothy 3:16
4. Call: 2 Matthew 5:14
5. Cross: Luke 23:44–46
6. Dawn: Psalm 30:5; Matthew 6:27
7. Eat: Psalm 34:8; Proverbs 22:2
8. Evil: Genesis 3:4; Philippians 4:8
9. Family: Ruth 1:16; 1 John 4:19
10. Fire: Romans 5:3–4
11. Game: Ecclesiastes 3:4
12. Glory: Psalm 21:5
13. Gospel: Isaiah: 6:8–9
14. Grasp: Acts 2:24; John 3:16
15. Grief: John 11:35; John 14:27
16. Hand: Matthew 25:35–36
17. Happy: James 1:2
18. Being a Hero: Luke 23:46
19. Hope: Jeremiah 29:12
20. Lamb: John 1:29
21. Life: Hebrews 11:3
22. Maker: Isaiah 43:25; Luke 13:24
23. Off: 2 Timothy 1:7
24. Pray: Matthew 21:22
25. Preach: 2 Timothy 4:2
26. Rock: Psalm 94:22; Psalm 68:19
27. Salt: Colossians 4:6
28. Sing: Psalm 63:7
29. Strong: Romans 12:12
30. Wept: Genesis 45:2
31. Yes: Genesis 6:22; Matthew 1:24; and Isaiah 1:19

"Scripture taken from the New American Standard Bible®, copyright 1960, 1962, 1963, 1968, 1971, 1972, 1973, 1975, 1977, 1995 by The Lockman Foundation. Used by permission."

Introduction

Adventures in Seeking Knowledge is my testimony of God's grace in my life through good times and bad times. This devotional shares with readers the moment God became very real and active in my heart and in my life. This collection of stories is a visual way to share my encounters with God's faithfulness. My goals are to encourage readers and provide moments of laughter along the way.

God won't ask everyone to write a book, compose a song, or create artwork in order to celebrate what He has done in their lives. But we're all asked to share in some way about God's grace, love, and faithfulness in our lives.

Thank you for the privilege of sharing my testimony with you!

Anger

Actions
Not
Graceful or
Easily
Redeemed after Display

"He who restrains his words has knowledge, And he who has a cool spirit is a man of understanding."
—*Proverbs 17:27*

It's uncomfortable to admit that at times I've got a temper.

Sometimes it may be on a day I just don't feel good. Sometimes it may be when I want to prove myself right it in a friendly debate. Neither of those things justify anger.

Does that sound familiar to anyone else?

Whenever I show this side of myself, it makes me feel horrible inside and out. Embarrassment creeps in, and in the heat of the moment, I bark out an insincere "I'm sorry." Then I have to retreat and sincerely apologize.

Adventures in Seeking Knowledge

My beloved and longtime pastor has done a series on family. His second sermon was on kindness. He said, "Kindness is a personal responsibility."

This statement holds a lot of powerful truth. We're responsible for how we respond to everyone in every situation.

Whether we believe we're justified in our anger at that moment doesn't really matter. What matters is how our anger will ultimately make someone else feel. We need to remember how we have felt when we've experienced anger from others.

Anger is never easy to handle, and it isn't easily redeemed.

Only God can redeem an angry spirt.

If you or someone you know suffers from anger, pray daily for God to provide peace. Seek counseling if the anger continues. There is hope!

Ask

Adventures
in
Seeking
Knowledge

"For the Lord gives wisdom; From His mouth come knowledge and understanding."
—*Proverbs 2:6*

    I've always enjoyed pretty notebooks and pens and all that comes with that, but learning didn't come easily for me. I often required one-on-one tutoring throughout my scholastic career. I would like to thank each teacher who took extra time with me. It's because of your dedication that I'm an avid bookworm, student of the written word, and an intellectually curious person. My quest for knowledge, however, has turned into nurturing a mature knowledge of the Word of God.

    I grew up in church, but it wasn't until I was an adult that Christ came into my heart. If you're still praying for someone to accept Christ, I pray that this will encourage you. I've come to learn that when Christ comes into your heart as an adult, He has work for you to do for Him.

Today God has become my master teacher. He's teaching me that He does have the best plan for my life. He's teaching me daily that He is my best friend, my main source of comfort, and my truest inspiration. He's teaching me to appreciate everything that life offers, even the good and the bad. He's teaching me to laugh more often and to not worry about tomorrow. Wow! What a great teacher!

What are some things God has taught you that you can share with others?

Bible

Bright
Inspirational
Books of
Love for
Everyone

"All Scripture is inspired by God and profitable for teaching, for reproof, for correction, for training in righteousness."
—*2 Timothy 3:16*

Numerous churches participate in Bible study, and they set aside a Sunday to give elementary students a Bible. How excited they are when they receive those Bibles for the first time! Then, at graduation, some churches present their students with a new Bible they can use through college and beyond.

Several churches participate in teaching scripture memorization or Bible drills to their children. Scripture teaches us to raise our children up on the Word of God. The earlier we introduce our children to God's Word, the more it will be imprinted in their minds and in their

Adventures in Seeking Knowledge

hearts. Such great knowledge of scripture will help them throughout life.

The overall theme of the Bible is the wondrous love of God and how He sent His son, Jesus, to die for our sins so we may spend eternity in Heaven with Him.

As an adult, I've come to appreciate all that the Bible has to offer. The Bible is a treasure chest of daily encouragement, love, and wisdom. The Bible is full of people who have experienced faith, forgiveness, grace, hope, love, mercy, patience, redemption, regret, sorrow, trials, and victories! In other words, they are a lot like us!

What are some of your special memories of getting your first Bible, and what are some of your favorite passages?

Call

Christ
Asking You to
Live as the
Light

"You are the light of the world. A city set on a hill cannot be hidden."
—*Matthew 5:14*

I received my two greatest blessings during my adult years.

The first occurred when I asked Christ into my heart. I've learned that when adults ask God into their hearts and into their lives, He's definitely got work for them to do!

The second—best thing in my life was a call to ministry that I received during a Women of Joy Conference. This wasn't on the calendar for me that particular year, but it quickly became obvious that I was supposed to be there. These two events have changed my heart, and this book is a result of those experiences.

Adventures in Seeking Knowledge

We will all be asked to serve God at some point in our relationship with Him. At first that thought made me nervous, but now I'm excited about all the possibilities. What are some possibilities presented to you?

As Christians, we should serve one another, our families, and our communities.

In addition to service, we may get opportunities to share our testimony. I still have a shaky voice when I share mine, but my confidence has grown, and yours will too!

Have any of your experienced a call to ministry and what does that involve for you?

Thanks to everyone who serves in Christ and for Christ!

Cross

Christ
Redeeming
Our
Souls through
Salvation

"It was now about the sixth hour, and darkness fell over the whole land until the ninth hour, because the sun was obscured; and the veil of the temple was torn in two. And Jesus, crying out with a loud voice, said, "Father, INTO YOUR HANDS I COMMIT MY SPIRIT." Having said this, He breathed His last."
—Luke 23:44–46

Let's slowly read these sentences together. Clear your mind, close your eyes, and try to picture the scenes being played out. Let's look at these precious truths:

- Jesus knew about God's plan for Him, yet He chose to endure the cross, the pain, and the death.
- Jesus died for me and for you.
- He died because we all have a Heaven to gain and a hell to shun.

- The veil was torn into from top to bottom.
- He was crucified between two thieves, and crucifixion was reserved for criminals.
- Pilate found no fault in Jesus, and neither do I.
- He was placed in a borrowed tomb.
- Three days later He arose!

Every time I read scriptures or hear sermons discussing this part of Jesus's life, I learn something new. Having a true understanding of this has caused my worship to be more active, and it has created a longing in me to learn more.

Read the different accounts in Matthew, Mark, Luke, and John. Pray for new insight as you read.

Dawn

Daylight
Awakening
When
Night Ends

*"For His anger is but for a moment, His favor is for a lifetime;
Weeping may last for the night, but a shout of joy comes
in the morning."*
—Psalm 30:5

Have you ever had one of those nights where you saw the changing of the clock every hour on the hour? Nights like these make us more tired than we went to bed.

I've experienced my share of those nights,
as I'm sure you have too.

When the day is done, and I have time to think, nagging thoughts come at me like a train going full speed ahead. These aggravating thoughts take the place of where praise should be, but I still allow myself to have them.

My mind starts to wonder about our finances, my health, and my loved ones.

Things I can't control—oh me!

I wonder if I've hurt anyone's feelings that day.

These thoughts can't and won't accomplish anything—namely, sleep!

As Matthew 6:27 says, "And who of you by being worried can add a *single* hour to his life."

I've known this scripture for a long time, but I need to apply it in my own life.

What keeps you up at night? What are some ways that help you sleep?

Remember when we were young, and counting sheep helped us sleep? Let's try counting our blessings; we will feel better rested in the morning!

Eat

Everything
at the
Table

*"O taste and see that the L*ORD *is good; How blessed is the man who takes refuge in Him!"*
—*Psalm 34:8*

During my last couple of mission trips, we've worked with homeless ministries in different cities. If you've never done this type of ministry, I challenge you to give it a try. This always gives me a fresh perspective and helps me recognize true blessings. Peace, love, and faithfulness are just a few examples of His goodness.

I've learned that every single person has a story, and it doesn't matter what your economic status may be. The person with the biggest mansion has a story of working their way up the corporate ladder or being born into a wealthy family.

When I've spoken with some of the homeless people and heard their stories, it never fails to touch my heart.

Adventures in Seeking Knowledge

Some may have become homeless due to natural disasters or a weak economy. Sadly, the possibilities are endless.

But, as Proverbs 22:2 tells us, "The rich and the poor have a common bond,
The LORD is the maker of them all."

Not only is the Lord the maker of all but He wants to

- be your friend,
- be a refuge for us,
- know that He is good,
- be filled with His words, and
- use us to show Jesus to the world.

What good things have you experienced from the Lord?

Ask Him for opportunities to share His goodness.

Evil

Every
Vicious and
Intentional
Lie

The serpent said to the woman, "You surely will not die!"
—Genesis 3:4

In the book of Genesis, we learn about all the beauty God created. We also see the first lie recorded—Satan's deception of Eve. Adam and Eve were given complete permission to enjoy everything God had created, with exception of one tree. It was all going smoothly; then Satan appeared and lied to Eve, which went against what God had said.

Eve listened to a lie instead of the truth. Now, I can't shake my head at Eve, because I often do the same thing. I listen to other things, just like Eve did, and because I'm not perfect, this is an easy trap for me to fall into.

Then there are lies that I tell myself: "I'm not pretty. I'm not good at anything. I shouldn't be writing."

Adventures in Seeking Knowledge

Every time I do this to myself, I'm totally discrediting God by saying His creation of me was not good. These lies we tell ourselves are vicious because we have to be built back up every time we tear ourselves down.

Let's close by reading Philippians 4:8, known as the "Whatsoever" verse:

- true
- honorable
- right
- pure
- lovely
- good repute
- things worthy of praise

These are the thoughts we need to practice dwelling on daily.

Try to find time each day to say something positive about yourself and those you encounter.

Family

Fellowship
Adventures
Ministry
Intentional
Love for
You

But Ruth said, "Do not urge me to leave you or turn back from following you; for where you go, I will go, and where you lodge, I will lodge. Your people shall be my people, and your God, my God."
—*Ruth 1:16*

Family is definitely my favorite blessing on earth. Families can be some of your best friends, your best cheerleaders, and your best prayer warriors.

Some of my favorite family and church family memories are as follows: family trips, holidays, ladies' ministry, mission trips, and vacation Bible school.

In my immediate family and family from marriage, I'm blessed with knowing our families will help each other.

Adventures in Seeking Knowledge

Fellowship of our families is imperative to building strong relationships and increasing your chances of spreading the gospel.

Ministry in families can also happen, and I believe when God sees this, He truly rejoices. Two of my favorite Bible women are Ruth and Naomi. My favorite part of this story is when Ruth tells Naomi that she will go wherever she goes after they had both endured hardships.
What love they show for each other as they go from family to devoted friendship.

Finally, the best gift of any family is love! 1 John 4:19 says, "We love, because He first loved us."

The older I get, the more I appreciate my family and my friends, who have turned into my family.

Take time today to pray for each family member, and find ways to encourage them.

Fire

Fierce and
Intense
Realities We Sometimes
Encounter

*"And not only this, but we also exult in our tribulations,
knowing that tribulation brings about perseverance; and
perseverance, proven character; and proven character, hope."*
—*Romans 5: 3–4*

- that dreaded 2:00 a.m. phone call that has bad news
  - a life-changing diagnosis
    - strained relationships
    - death of a loved one
    - financial burdens

These are just some of the things that I've experienced that have put my faith to the test, and God has used to help me learn how to depend on Him.

Some of these things may be familiar to you too.

Whenever I encounter trials of any kind, I continue to learn about the faithfulness, goodness, and mercy of God.

Adventures in Seeking Knowledge

I've always been one who has to learn the hard way, but it's these instances that help my relationship with God grow to a deeper and more personal level.

Let's look at how God tested Jesus's faith:

- betrayal
- followers who had gone astray
- difficult ministry because it was His Father's will
- an extremely painful and humiliating death

Even though Jesus's life was filled with extremely difficult challenges, He cherished the promises of His Father.

The good news is, we can too!

When our faith is put to the fire, God provides comfort, friendship, grace, guidance, hope, love, mercy, peace, rest, and strength.

What are some blessings you've received from God when life became difficult, and how can you encourage others with your story?

Game

Giggles
Action
Meals
Entertainment

"A time to weep and a time to laugh; a time to mourn and a time to dance."
—*Ecclesiastes 3:4*

Even when we were dating, Sammy and I loved to play board games and card games for our date nights. As a married couple, we've had numerous game nights at our home with our friends, who are definitely like family to us. If you've ever experienced game night with me and come back again, then you're my true friend!

During our game night fellowships, I have a comedy routine with a mutual friend. Out of brotherly love, we engage in smack talk that equals no other, and everyone listens intently to see what we might say.

Through these special gatherings, this group has learned my strengths and weaknesses. They endure my love of one-liners and knock-knock jokes. They know that Sammy and I enjoy opening our home for fellowship.

These are the ones who help us when life gets hard and celebrate with us when times are good.

When this group puts all our talents together, we work toward a common goal of growing in our faith and serving others. This is how your small group can grow. Start out meeting regularly, away from church, and then break out into fellowship and ministry.

Fellowship nights can also help your group identify possible ministry needs. Offer a fellowship night for your small group, and I promise you'll laugh and learn about someone in a different light.

Glory

God's
Love
Offering a
Relationship with
You

"His glory is great through Your salvation, Splendor and Majesty You place upon Him."
—*Psalm 21:5*

At Christmastime, my spirit is filled with childlike excitement! I love the Christmas baking, decorations, lights, parties, programs, and the Christmas shopping!

This year, however, I encountered—and felt humbled by—a different level of excitement at Christmastime. That gift is being in awe of God's glory!

God displayed His glory to me this year by

- becoming my friend and my provider;
- being able to see spiritual growth in family members, friends, and myself;
- bringing hope and peace to a hurting heart;

- giving me things to laugh about during life's trials;
- seeing and experiencing relationship restoration; <u>and</u>
  - witnessing and hearing stories of healing from loved ones.

Best of all, I've seen God's glory in *truly* coming to understand the uniqueness of Jesus's birth, the power of the cross, and the redemptive grace of His resurrection!

Finally, I've learned the passion that Jesus has in wanting a relationship with me and you! This new enlightenment is what helps me get through those hard days, has made me appreciate myself and others more, and has helped me understand grace! Jesus doesn't want any wrapped gifts from us. He wants our hearts, our love, and our time.

My prayer is that you find excitement in knowing that God desires a relationship with you and that you're able to see God's glory in your everyday routine.

Gospel

Great
Opportunities to
Share with
People the
Eternal
Love of God

Then I heard the voice of the Lord saying, "Whom shall I send and who will go for us?" Then I said, "Here, I am, send me".
—Isaiah 6:8–9

What a great attitude from the prophet Isaiah! There was no hesitation in his response, and he bravely reported for duty without knowing all the details of the assignment. If we could all catch his excitement, think of how many people would be introduced to Jesus through our work as missionaries.

I have been on several different mission trips, so I know something about the time it takes to prepare, plan, and pray. But we also know some career missionaries, and to me, they are some of the bravest people I know. They give up their comfort zones, time with their families and friends, and safe surroundings to spread God's Word. We truly thank all of you!

But we don't have to go far away to do mission work. Most of the time, right where we are is where we have the greatest potential to do God's work. We just have to be available to act and be courageous enough to obey God's calling. Great are the rewards for those who go in Jesus's name.

Have you ever been on a mission trip? Write a story or draw pictures that details your mission experiences. Share it often. Your story may encourage a future missionary.

Grasp

God's
Redemption
Allows
Salvation to All
People

"But God raised Him up again, putting an end to the agony of death, since it was impossible for Him to be held in its power!"
—*Acts 2:24*

On this beautiful Easter Sunday, let's look at the third word listed: *allows*! It seems that I'm in this beautiful season of being able to *grasp* more than ever all that God has allowed to be done for me. Knowing that this is available for everyone excites me!

I'm beginning to understand the extreme importance of a verse I learned in childhood, John 3:16: "For God so loved the world that He gave His only begotten Son that whoever believes in Him shall not perish but have eternal life." This verse deserves to be said with reverence because this is where it all began!

Adventures in Seeking Knowledge

Because of God's love, He gave His Son, Jesus, to all who call upon His name! God allows Jesus to be our strength. I'm thankful that God allows Jesus to be active in our lives

God allows Jesus to be our comforter, encourager, friend, helper, mediator, and teacher! God allowed His son, Jesus, to die on the cross so we can live in Heaven for eternity.

God has become my father, friend, encourager, healer, my salvation, and the one I trust. He is allowing my relationship to deepen with Him!

What has God allowed Jesus to be for you during different seasons of life?

Grief

Great
Remorse That
Impacts
Everyone's
Feelings

"Jesus Wept."

—John 11:35

Unfortunately, grief is something we all face. The main cause of grief is usually the loss of a loved one.

When I encounter grief, I don't handle it well. I want to block out those who care about me the most by not talking about the matters of my heart. I brush aside any offers of help. I've learned that journaling is a great coping skill.

Jesus had plenty to weep about during His life. He knew the plan that God had for Him on the cross. He knew What His loved ones would see with His horrific death. He knew about the sins of the world and how many still needed to come to Him in faith.

Adventures in Seeking Knowledge

"Peace I leave with you; My peace I give to you; not as the world gives do I give to you. Do not let your heart be troubled, nor let it be fearful."

—*John 14:27*

This is one of the most comforting verses that helps me when I experience a painful season of grief. I'm thankful that God knew we would all encounter grief in our life, and He prepared for the Holy Spirt to be our comforter, friend, healer, and listener.

What are some of your verses that you go to when life brings you grief? These verses would be good to put on index cards to commit to memory.

Hand

Helping
All in
Need
Daily

"For I was hungry, and you gave Me something to eat; I was thirsty, and you gave Me something to drink; I was a stranger, and you invited Me in; naked, and you clothed Me; I was sick, and you visited Me; I was in prison, and you came to Me."
—*Matthew 25:35–36*

I'm blessed to have parents who have a generous spirit and are always willing to serve! Some of my childhood memories are of Mom and Dad reaching out to those in their church, their work families, and the community to lend a helping hand. Generosity begins at home.

There are different seasons of needs that we can and will face in life. Some of these needs may be emotional, financial, and physical. Our emotional needs can be helped through a counselor or caring friend with a listening ear. Financial and physical needs can often be met just by being willing to help out. I love seeing communities come together to help no matter what the need may be. This is truly Christ in action!

We can all be a part of God's work of helping each other just by training our eyes to be more aware of what's going on around us. We never know when we may be the one needing a helping hand.

What are some ways you can help your community or church to be daily missionaries?

What are some organizations that are good community outreach sources?

Happy

Having
Amazingly
Pleasant
Peace inside
You

"Count it all joy, my brethren, when you encounter various trials."
—*James 1:2*

I recently had the privilege of attending a special-called prayer service for a church member who had been diagnosed with a medical condition. I had the intention of going to pray for this sweet family. I ended up, however, being blessed by the one enduring the sickness. He bravely got up and spoke about what God has brought him through and what he knows God will bring him and his family through. Then he shared something God had whispered in his heart, and it hit me hard. The statement was, "Be happy with where you are."

What a brave thing to share! I've been a Christian for a long time now, and my level of happiness has not reached this yet. My happiness often depends on my circumstances, like the balance in our checking account or if I have weekend plans or if I'll be able to finish my Christmas shopping early!

None of these things even begin to define happiness.

Happiness is spending time in the word and learning about your savior. Happiness is having a community of believers who enjoy life with you. Happiness is realizing that God will never leave you or forsake you.

Happiness is a growing personal relationship with God!

Happiness equals peace!

Sing this playful song, "If You're Happy and You Know It." This song always makes me smile!

Embrace happiness every day!

Being a Hero

Happens Somewhere
Every Day despite
Risky
Obstacles

"And Jesus, crying out with a loud voice, said, "Father, into Your hands I commit My Spirit." Having said this, He breathed His last."
—Luke 23:46

I'm a big-time supporter of men and women who serve our great nation in career fields that help save lives! I'm extremely thankful for our fearless military, police force, firefighters, paramedics, doctors, and nurses who work hard day in and day out to help save lives. They go through a long process of academic and physical training to be able to help in dire times of need.

Then there's our ultimate hero, Jesus Christ! With His extremely humble background, how His life played out for everyone makes Him a hero.

- Born in a manger among animals and was worshiped by royalty at birth.
  - Healed the sick and resurrected the dead.
- Jesus knew He would endure betrayal; hunger and poverty; temptation; beatings, mockery, and abuse; and a crown of thorns.

Jesus Christ is a hero because He died an extremely painful death on the cross for me and you to save us from an eternal hell! Has there been a time in your life when you've accepted Jesus as your savior? If you haven't, please invite Him into your heart and into your life today. He will become your Hero!

Take some time this week to personally thank the local heroes who help protect us every day.

Hope

Hearing
Our
Prayers
Every Day and Everywhere

*"Then you will call upon Me and come and pray to Me,
and I will listen to you."*
—*Jeremiah 29:12*

The confidence we have in knowing that God hears our prayers and has a desire for us to talk to Him is what gets me through those days of

- being consumed by anxiety,
  - confusion,
  - depression,
  - feeling helpless,
  - distress, and
  - grief

Can I get an amen?

Even in those times I thought God wasn't listening to me, I knew He was really being active on my behalf.

Sometimes He answers us with yes, no, or not now, but we can rejoice knowing that God is listening

The Bible is full of stories of how God listens to the cries of our hearts:

- Joseph and his journey from slavery to freedom.
- Esther and her cry to save her people.
- Hannah and her cry to have a child.

These are just a few of my favorites.

In these examples, He heard and listened to what His children were saying to Him. He still answers prayers today. Every time He answers our prayers, we should show gratitude to Him and remember that He does listen to us. Are you in a deep season of prayer in your life now? Can you remember times when God had answered your prayers? Take time to thank God often for those answered prayers, and ask God for opportunities to share your testimonies of answered prayers.

Lamb

Love
and
Mercy through His
Blood

The next day he saw Jesus coming to him and said, "Behold, the Lamb of God who takes away the sin of the world!"
—*John 1:29*

The lamb is one of the most popular animals in the Bible.

One of my favorite pictures growing up is a huge picture of Jesus holding a lamb and lambs sitting all around Him.

We see in the story of Abraham where he goes to offer up his son Isaac as a sacrifice that God provides a lamb instead.

The Lamb is also used when the altars were built, and the people searched for a spotless lamb to be used as a sacrifice on the altar.

God performed the same miracle for us. He sent us the lamb to die in our place on the cross. Through His blood, we experience forgiveness, freedom, hope, mercy, life, and love!

The lamb—an innocent and spotless animal that served such a huge purpose for us all. God can use any and all of His creation to fulfill purposes for Him.

I'm so thankful that God sent the lamb of Christ to take our place—to die for our sins, to love us unconditionally, to comfort and guide us, and to heal our hearts.

What are some things you're thankful for that the blood of the lamb provides for you? What are some of your favorite scriptures that talk about the sacrifices that God made for us?

Life

Living
in
Faith
Every Day

"By <u>faith</u> we <u>understand</u> that the <u>worlds</u> were <u>prepared</u> by the <u>word</u> of <u>God</u>, <u>so</u> that what is <u>seen</u> was not <u>made</u> out of things which are <u>visible</u>."
—Hebrews 11:3

Faith is a small word with a huge meaning.

The power of faith in Christ has the miraculous outcome of establishing your home in Heaven.

Faith in Christ will always get you through the toughest of days, and faith can heal the hurting heart.

We're blessed to have people in our life who demonstrate living out their faith. For me, it started with my parents, Don and Pam, both of whom have a strong personal relationship with Christ. God blessed me with my husband, Sammy, who is truly a man of faith.

Adventures in Seeking Knowledge

Finally, their faith became my own!

I realized that I believed in the life, the death, and the resurrection of Jesus Christ.

I changed over time. I started getting interested in the Word of God. I began to seek these things more than ever, and I felt the desire to share His Word.

Now I have my faith in Christ to help uphold me when I get a message that may bring bad news. My faith upholds me when I feel alone or overwhelmed. My faith calms me and reminds me that God always fulfills our needs.

What are some things your faith has helped you overcome?

Maker

Master Builder of
a Heavenly
Kingdom for
Everyone Who
Repents

"I, even I, am the one who wipes out your transgressions for My own sake, And I will not remember your sins."
—*Isaiah 43:25*

This scripture paints a beautiful picture of how God extends His forgiveness to us when we repent. He promises that He will not remember our sins, and I have it on good authority that He is a promise keeper!

Luke gives us a warning that should make us ensure our salvation: "Strive to enter through the narrow door; for many, I tell you, will seek to enter and will not be able" (Luke 13:24).

Scripture from Romans provides us an illustration of repentance: "That if you confess with your mouth Jesus *as* Lord, and believe in your heart that God raised Him from

Adventures in Seeking Knowledge

the dead, you will be saved; for with the heart a person believes, resulting in righteousness, and with the mouth he confesses, resulting in salvation" (Romans 10:9–10).

If you're reading this page and realize that this is something you need to do, please know that I'm celebrating your decision! I, too, made a decision for Christ as an adult! I'd love to hear some of your testimonies of Christ and how He came into your life.

Please contact a church staff member and let them know about your decision. Your church family will want to celebrate your decision, and they will also encourage you as you grow!

Congratulations! I'm proud of you!

Off

Openly
Facing Your
Fears

"For God has not given us a spirt of timidity, but of power and love and discipline."
—*2 Timothy 1:7*

One of my fears is diving boards, because dog-paddling is the best swimming I can do. One summer my husband and I were at a friend's house, and I decided I was going to jump off the deep end. Sammy got in the deep end to wait and watch.

I jumped! It wasn't graceful, but I jumped. The next thing I know, my head popped up above the water, and Sammy cheered for me. My fear of the diving board had been faced, and nothing happened. I haven't done that again. It's not because I'm afraid—that just isn't my idea of fun.

Most fears, however, are much bigger than my fear of jumping off a diving board.

Adventures in Seeking Knowledge

Some people who have experienced a natural disaster, like hurricanes and tornadoes, have justifiable fear of those storms. Someone who has poor employment history might fear being fired. As I worked on this book, I feared losing my manuscript several times! If we're not careful, fear can prevent us from enjoying life.

We serve a God who will calm our fears and give us the courage to face them. God will also provide with us support groups to help us face our fears.

Can you recall a victory in your life when God helped you overcome fear?

Pray

Providing
Real
Answers for
You

"And all things you ask in prayer, believing, you will receive."
—Matthew 21:22

The biblical principle of prayer has been debated a lot in my lifetime. I'm thankful, though, that as Christians, there's no debate that we have the privilege to talk to God through prayer.

We can pray standing up, sitting down, driving, on the job, in a classroom, or in the hospital. We can pray out loud, silently, or we can write our prayers. It doesn't matter which positions our physical bodies are in while we pray, but the condition of our spirits does matter. Scripture tells us that prayers won't be heard if you have unbelief, hate, evil, or greed in your heart.

I'm guilty of praying selfishly. For example, if there was something, I wanted that I thought was best for me,

Adventures in Seeking Knowledge

I would exclaim, "Yes, I prayed about it!" I wouldn't admit, though, that I'd given God the freedom to answer the prayer His way. I've personally learned that rushing God will never turn out in your best interest. None of my selfish prayers have worked the way I had planned.

I've also heard many times that God has three way in which to answer our prayers. The answers are *yes*, *no*, or *wait*. *Yes* is more often what we want to hear, but when God answers *no* or *wait*, sometimes that's a blessing in disguise.

What are you currently praying about, and who could be your prayer partner?

Preach

Proclaiming
Realities about
Eternity and
Changing
Hearts

"Preach the word; be ready in season and out of season; reprove, rebuke, exhort, with great patience and instruction."
—*2 Timothy 4:2*

All of us haven't been called to preach the Word of God, but those who claim that Christ lives in our hearts and in our lives are called to teach and share the Word of God.

I've been blessed to have a life that is influenced by good preachers who are godly men, not only in our churches but also in their homes and our community. These preachers also promote unity in our state and worldwide as we partner to work with other churches.

I've been blessed to have heard words of biblical inspiration, instruction, and correction from every church I've been associated with as a member.

Adventures in Seeking Knowledge

Below are just a few gems I've learned from preachers who have impacted my life:

- "Don't let all that people hear from you about what Jesus has done in your life be in past tense."
- "Jesus can be your best friend."
- "Your life doesn't have to be perfect to come to Jesus."
- "Strive to be more like Jesus today than you were yesterday."

Another truth I've learned is that we are called as individuals and a church family to help ministers carry out the role of the church in our community and to spread the Gospel.

Let's actively look for ways to:

- pray for our ministers and their families; and
- encourage, serve, and thank them.

Rock

Resting
Our
Cares in
King Jesus

"But the Lord has been my stronghold, And my God the rock of my refuge."
—*Psalm 94:22*

I'm a worrier. Are any of you like that too? I try hard not to worry, but it's a constant battle.

Psalm 68:19 paints a beautiful picture of one of the great things that God does for us. It states: "Blessed be the Lord, who daily bears our burden, The God of our salvation."

God knew that life would be challenging, and we would have burdens, heartaches, worries, and troubles. We can try to give those to our family and friends, which I often do, but the Lord is the best One to handle our worries.

When we learn to truly spend daily time with God, we can have more peace and rest than when we try to carry our cares on our own. Our friends may be busy, but as a believer, God is always with you and ready to hear from you.

Our Lord is able and willing to be our stronghold and refuge. We only need to let Him be that for us. When we give our troubles to Jesus, we know that they are being handled by the greatest possible hands.

What burdens do you need to give to Jesus today that will allow you to rest better and walk with less weight on your shoulders? Take time daily to spend with Jesus, and please pray that I will do that too.

Salt

Speaking and
Living the
Truth

"Let your speech always be with grace, as though seasoned with salt, so that you will know how you should respond to each person."
—*Colossians 4:6*

Salt has many purposes. It adds flavor to our food, and our bodies must maintain a certain level of salt. When the weather is icy, the public works departments use salt to help us drive safely.

Just as salt is necessary in different areas, salt is referred to in the Bible as being a proper way to live. The Bible is full of scriptures that teach us how to behave in conduct and in speech. Our actions always speak louder than our words, but our words still affect how we represent Jesus.

The book of James discusses how quickly the tongue can spread things like wildfire, ultimately bringing destruction.

Destruction could be in the form of your reputation, someone else's reputation, or a business or family situation.

Being someone who has had experiences with gossip, I know both ends and how painful that can be! Thankfully, as I grow in the Lord, I'm more aware of gossip and try my best to avoid it.

I believe that when our words are seasoned with the salt, then our actions will comply, and our witness for God will be protected. I'm working on developing a discipline of stop, think, and pray before speaking.

What are some things that can help salt our words daily and effectively?

Sing

Sharing
Inspirational
Notes about
God's Love

"For You have been my help, and in the shadow of Your wings I sing for joy."
—Psalm 63:7

Today my pastor talked about why, as Christians, it's important for us to sing. He stated that Christianity is a singing religion, and it's part of our DNA to sing. Singing is one of my favorite parts of church.

What do we have to sing about? What do I have to sing about?

Well, we may not have the same answers, because our stories are different, but for me, I sing because

- Jesus has come into my heart and life;
- Jesus has become my best friend;
- Jesus has helped me endure a season of depression and healed my hurting heart;

Adventures in Seeking Knowledge

- Jesus has comforted me numerous times;
- Jesus is the provider of all that I need; and
- Jesus died on the cross for me and you to rescue us from an eternity in hell.

This is just a small list of reasons why I'm blessed to be able to sing traditional church songs as well as our more contemporary music. I'm never going to win a Grammy for my singing or be asked to sing a solo, but I sing because it's a part of worship. We sing because it's one way to express our gratitude to God. Where can we sing? Anywhere and everywhere!

Take some time this week to play and sing some of your favorite worship songs and hymns!

Strong

Steadfast
Trusted
Resilient
Obedient
Near to
God

"Rejoicing in hope, preserving in tribulation, devoted to prayer."
—Romans 12:12

I'm going to reverse things here and do the application first.
Take time out, please, and go look in your mirror.
I'll wait a few minutes.

OK, good—thanks for humoring me.

Chances are high that the strong person I've just described is the person you are looking at in the mirror.

That's right—that strong person is *you*!

I believe every one of us has a story, or multiple stories, that have made us into the strong people we are today. You've had to do something all by yourself for the first time, or you've faced an extreme sickness, or you've faced other adventures of the unknown. These stories, however, are what has made me personally know that I can rely on God at all times. Change is constant in life, but I've learned that "Jesus Christ is the same yesterday and today and forever." (Hebrews 13:8).

God has blessed me with having the privilege of knowing some very strong men and women in my life. They display the ability to bounce back. They enjoy helping others, even when they are hurting themselves. They have the gift of sharing their stories. They choose to rely on the strength of Jesus instead of their own.

These people have greatly impacted my faith, my life, and my writing.

What are some of your stories, and who are some people who made you strong?

Wept

When
Events Finally
Produce
Tears

"He wept so loudly that the Egyptians heard it, and the household of Pharaoh heard of it."
—*Genesis 45:2*

I don't cry often. But when I finally cry, I break! No one likes to cry, but it's a necessary part of healing.

Have you ever cried until you were worn-out?

The story of Joseph's life is one of my favorites. He went through some extremely challenging and difficult times, but he held true to his faith in God. This story demonstrates how God can use our pain for His glory!

Joseph's brothers sold him into slavery. Bible scholars say he was an early teen.

Adventures in Seeking Knowledge

Fast-forwarding to Joseph's later years, he became essential to Pharaoh and Egypt because of his ability to interpret dreams. Please read Genesis 41–50.

Joseph predicted the seven years of famine in Egypt. This is ultimately how God allowed him to rescue the very brothers who sold him into slavery!

Genesis 43 describes how Joseph fed the ones who betrayed him at his table. Talk about extreme forgiveness and not bringing up past offenses!

It's after this scene that Joseph finally allowed himself to weep so loudly that the Egyptians heard it, and Pharaoh's household heard him weeping. I can't fully imagine what the sheer volume of that cry was, but I can imagine that healing began for Joseph.

Do you have something you need to cry about today? Please don't hold it in. Remember that God loves you!

Yes

Yielding
Everything to Our
Savior

"Thus, Noah did; according to all that God had commanded him, so he did."
—*Genesis 6:22*

The Bible has numerous examples of people who exercised extreme obedience and left legacies for generations to come.

Noah is the first one who comes to mind when we talk about obedience. His story of the ark illustrates that obedience to God is something that happens at all ages. Noah was approximately 120 years old when he completed building the ark. Yet he was obedient by completing the ark and warning people of the rain and destruction that was to come. This resulted in the protection of his family.

In Matthew 1:24, we see where Joseph awoke from a dream and did what the Lord commanded him and took Mary as his wife. God knew that Mary and Joseph would ultimately do what was asked of them. He looked upon them with high favor. This obedience has extreme significance throughout all history—down to our personal salvation from the Lord.

Isaiah 1:19 states, "If you consent and obey, you will eat from the best of the land." Isiah is reminding his people, whom he was trying to help, that obedience results in what is in your best interest. Obedience is always the best road to take, and it will always produce positive results for you.

What are some stories of obedience that have impacted your life, and how can obedience become easier to practice?

Bibliography

Rose Hale lives in the beautiful state of Alabama, with her husband, Sammy. *Adventures in Seeking Knowledge* is a devotional book about her faith in God with personal stories that have helped my faith grow.

She has published two children's books under the pen name Anna Daily, *Blessings for Betsy and Betsy Goes to Church*.

When she's not writing, she enjoys playing with their dog, TJ; spending time with her family and her friends; and reading and photography.

www.ingramcontent.com/pod-product-compliance
Lightning Source LLC
Chambersburg PA
CBHW050043080526
44586CB00014B/1440